FAIL FALL FLY

FAITH OVER FAILURE

BISMA AYOUB NAJAR

DEDICATING THIS BOOK TO EVERYONE OUT THERE,

WHO

FAILED,

FELL,

AND

FLIED.

Contents

Contents

Foreword

Here is the young and talented Author BISMA AYOUB with her another brilliant and mesmerizing book 'FAIL, FALL AND FLY.

After having a successful and lovely journey with her award winning book 'THE CREATIVE MINDS' and Mukhtasar (A Short Journey Of Pain) udoubtdly this one is also going to be a masterpiece.

You will fall in love with her thoughts and the experiences shared in this book as they will give you all a broader vision of seeing imperfect life with utmost perfection. Despite being a good Author and a Public Speaker BISMA has always been or tried to be there for the society and the fellow artists which makes her different from the rest.

BISMA is gifted with skillful writing and her style of writing simple and raw which allows her to go straight to the hearts. The art of putting emotions in her writing just simply not capture minds but souls.

After being asked to read some chapters and give some reviews for this book. Firstly I was overwhelmed as it is really proud and honour to write for such an renowed Author and secondly I would simply say it's a pure art of work. The way she has made us understand how with every negative phase comes a long lasting positivity is something we all need at certain times of our lives.

The strength of FAIL,FALL AND FLY lies in the magnificent ablity to present her story in a motivational manner. If you are defeated, broken, off track or disheartened this is the best read to find light, hope and desire. This is not just a book but a huge endowment to the society. It is surely going to motivate you and will empower your imagination. FAIL,FALL AND FLY is the best example of, why the Author finds her name in the Indian book of records.

"Fanoos banke jiski hifazat hawa kare,

Woh shama kya bhuje jise Roshan KHUDA kare"

(When the breeze protects the flame in the

form of a chimney,

None can turn off such a flame that is lit up by THE ALMIGHTY ALLAH)

Thank you for this amazing contribution.

For sure Bisma you have a bright and successful future. May allah shower his blessings on you and bless you with good health, May you achieve the heights of success and may your pen remains powerful and pure always.

Rise and shine.

******WELL WISHER******

Preface

"SOMETHINGS DON'T HAVE A REASON TO HAPPEN, THEY JUST HAPPEN BECAUSE THEY WERE MEANT TO". (BISMA AYOUB)

A girl who never wanted to know what life can be in the worst of its faces was suddenly brought to a place to experience it whole.

Bisma Ayoub, Author of 2 books and a WRITER for life, started penning down the emotions, feelings, love and mostly pain in her early age. Even not knowing what love means she used to write pain, may be because that is something she had seen most or experienced the most.

For her Writng is just like the other necessity of life, her life without pen and paper is incomplete.

She found her best companion within her notebooks, a companion who never complained, who never betrayed and who never gave upon her.

Writing this book has made her thoughts about life more clear and the reason of sharing this work is almost same. We all are living in a world where nothing goes unfiltered. We correct almost each and everything before making it public. Why?

Are we all afraid of being real in this fake world or the filters has took over the realistic life?

We want everything to be perfect, we correct pictures before posting, to make them look beautiful, we alter things not because we always want to alter them but because perfection is not there.

Is life Perfect?

Nothing is perefect. Even the picture used on the cover of this book is unedited. Because in the world where the essence of raw and real is losing I want to be real with myself. This book will help you all to realise that no matter how much we filter, alter and edit things, Life is going to be imperfect.

So we need to appreciate the imperfection to make our lives and thoughts beautiful.

We all need to live a imperfectly perfect life.

BISMA AYOUB

Acknowledgements

Alhamdulillah!

My utmost Shukur and gratitude towards the Almighty Allah, who once again blessed my pen to write for the third time (book) and always, few months back I was not expecting that i am going to make it, But Allah has his own plans and he gave me this life to live it in much much wiser way.

A special thanks to Mr Atul Joshi firstly for such amazing cover pictures, secondly for always being my constant support and well wisher.

My parents, my siblings (MUDASIR AYOUB & YUSRA AYOUB) for the supprt and encouragement you have shown at all the steps of my life. Wihtout you guys it was never possible.

My friends, readers, followers and everyone out there, who in one or the other way motivated me, inspired me to do better and best.

Thank you all for being so much supportive, loving and coperative....

Prologue

Here's how you fail: You fail with your heart on your sleeve.

You fail like you mean it with every part of you.

You fail attempting the impossible and the ridiculous.

You fail in front of others and you fail and they laugh at you and you fail and you feel nothing and regret less.

You fail sincerely and earnestly and you risk everything at every opportunity.

This is how you fail: You fail beautifully.

You fail with grace...

CHAPTER ONE

A GOLDEN DAY

Meow Meow Meow!

So here's the start to the amazing day with positive vibes all around and I was happy that finally after a long time everything seemed to be in place and at peace at the same time♥. And as usual, my morning started with ''Bismaaaaaaaa uthna Nahi hai, late hogaya doctor k pass b Jaana hai." My mom screamed from downstairs and I ignored her as I didn't want to come out of my bed in this chilly winter. But mum is mum and finally I was up. Knowing that it was going to be a hectic day I was all set to go with my Mum.

Waiting Waiting but no buses at all, here I used my Jagga Jasoos mind and looked for a cab and fortunately got one☺. So we had a good conversation with the driver too, like how he managed to start his car in the morning and the struggle he made to accept our ride ''Laughs''.

Wohoooooo finally at the doctor's place but oooooopsssssss we were late and had to wait for our turn which was after 10 people. It was going to be really really hard and boring at the same time. So me and Mum kept waiting in the hall , Mum looking at me and I looking into my phone''Laughs''. Wait What was I supposed to do there instead of being on my phone all the time?

Suddenly I looked at my Mum and she was trying to say something and she made all the efforts to make me understand but I am me and I failed to understand what she wanted to say. MY BAD. "LAUGHS". I ignored her for sometime but her actions were making me feel awkward and finally I understood what she was trying to say. And my Mum was having her craving for chai at its peak.

Let's go out and have Tea " MUM said".
Mama, what's wrong are we here to have tea?
But what are we going to do here because the doctor is going to take too much time, so let's move out and have tea. Her temptation and

motivational power at the same time made me to go out with her. She won because Mothers are the Winners. We came out and started a walk-in search of a DHABAAA nearby to calm down my MUM.

We reached near SHALIMAR GARDEN and fortunately found a DHABAA and I asked the worker, Do we have chai ? And yayyyyyyyyyyy we were good to go with the garrmaaa garam chai with crispy pakoras. We went inside to sit and while entering the place I saw a lady sitting there on a chair and having her tea. While we were grabbing our seats she said "KASHMIRI LOGON KO CHAI HONI HI CHAHIYE, CHAHY KUCH BHI HO. We all smiled and had a seat. She started a conversation with MUM and I felt a bit awkward but she seemed to be a great and intellectual lady. Meanwhile we got our tea and MUM was happy to see that.

What do you do? " The LADY asked".
I am a student and I do write sometimes, no actually, I try to write " I replied".
So now the conversation started and she was asking more about my profession and other things. She shared her experiences and I was shocked to know that the LADY was double M.A in English and B.A, B.ED. I was having a good time with her she was talking to my

MUM too and was talking about the life of LAL DED and her translations to her words made me move to the next world wherein I was connecting it all to Rasul Mir as I am working on his poetry.

"YE APKI BETI AAPKA NAAM BAHUT ROSHAN KREGI AUR YE APNI ZINDAGI MAI BAHUT TARAQI KAREGI " Lady said to my MUM".
AMEEN " My MUM replied".
Apki duaa honi chahiye " MUM added

She was not an ordinary lady, her words, facts, logics and the phrases with deep meanings were something that moved me. She was looking at me contineously and instead of being awkward I started to feel more comfortable as I too wanted to have more and more conversation with her.

And we were running late as we were having an appointment with the doctor.
Chalo fir Chaltay hai " MUM said".
Yesss we have to go " I replied".
So we got up to move out from that place and before leaving we shaked hands and while leaving the place she said" ALLAH APKO KAMIYAB KARE"
AMEEN.

She was a gem I understood a little later. Her words and advice motivated me to the next level. She was full of purity, love and innocence. While walking back towards the clinic MUM and me were discussing how this all started and how and where we were supposed to meet this pure lady.

For me, the day was already successful and my mood was even more stable and at peace.

"MORAL"
APPRECIATE THE ARRIVAL AND DEPARTURE OF PEOPLE IN YOUR LIFE. WHOSOEVER COMES IN YOUR LIFE THEY COME WITH CERTAIN LESSONS TO GIVE AND EXPERIENCES TO SHARE. APPRECIATE EACH ONE, APPRECIATE THEIR STAY AND THEIR LOSS. IN EITHER WAY WE ARE BLESSED TO LEARN, SHARE AND GROW.

CHAPTER TWO

EXPECT THE UNEXPECTED

Sometimes it's very hard to understand what's happening in life. Sometimes all you need is an escape from this world to the world where there is no one but you, only you all around.

I have lived and survived my life, I have witnessed all the ups and downs, I have gone through all the criticism one can ever face, I have been taunted and bullied by my closed ones, I have been taken to the skies and then thrashed away, I have been entertained and then ignored to the heights of pain.

YES... I have gone through all this...

There came a day in my life where everything was at the losing end, where all my dreams and fantasies were fading away, where all my actions were against my mind and soul, where I wasn't I any more but someone else. All I can say that I was in Depression, Yes you read it right DEPRESSION.

DEPRESSION is not something we must brag about, the new generation and the youth mostly use this word as swag but we must know what it actually is. Depression made me a person I never thought and imagined in my wildest dreams, it took me far away from my family, I lost my sweet smile, I lost my friends, I lost my mind, I lost my soul, I lost the reasons to live, I lost my dreams, I lost my confidence, I lost my creativeness, I lost MYSELF and that was the worst of all.

Losing yourself means you are half dead. It means you are surviving but not living, it means there is just a structure of muscles and bones with no soul in it. Losing yourself is worst and to be honest it is the time you die. I was dead because the Me in Me was lost. I started to find happiness in others, I started begging for the things that belong to me, I started struggling for the life I deserved. But there came a time where I understood a simple but the most important thing about life and that was " THERE WILL BE NO ONE BUT YOU, ONLY YOU WILL HELP YOURSELF".

This mantra changed my life, I can say that this was the turning point of my life. I realized very late that there was no one even when I was surrounded by many. It was only a myth that having many people around means you are happy and you have them by your side all the time. It's only you who is with you all the time and everywhere, only you can help yourself, only you can take care of yourself, only u can love yourself.

MORAL

CHERISH YOURSELF, LOVE YOURSELF, AND RESPECT YOURSELF. DON'T LOOK FOR HAPPINESS IN OTHERS, YOU CAN ONLY FIND THAT IN YOU. YOU ARE YOUR PRIDE. YOU ARE THE ONE AND ONLY. BE YOU AND BE YOUR BEST ALL THE TIME. WITH EVERY PASSING DAY YOU SEE, OBSERVE AND FLY HIGHER.

CHAPTER THREE

NO (AN ANSWER)

I woke up as a strong girl, a girl who needs no one but her own self. I saw myself in the mirror , I smiled and I was proud that at last I survived the hard and the tough part of my life. I was happy to see the new me in the old me. I was all ready to go and make my dreams a reality.

But we must remember that there are some people here on the earth who will never appreciate you, they will be waiting for you to make a mistake, they will be standing there to see you burn where you stand. And there will be you proving them wrong and flying higher and higher.

People like them are not capable of doing anything on their own, so they always try to be a barrier in between you and your dreams.

And trust me, all this happened with me also, when I tried to move on in my life, when I tried to be happy again, when I tried to step out from that zone where I was lost and dead.

There was a time where I felt that this is not going to work, I should not come out from my room, I should not talk to anyone ,I should not share my feelings and moreover I should not move on.

''BISMA you are getting late for your college'' , a voice striking my ears and yes it was my MUM calling me.

It took me a minute or so to realize that it was just a flashback, a flashback to the past, a flashback to the nightmare, a flashback which isn't worth remembering. But that flashback reminded me what i have to tackle in my life.

I was still standing in-front of the mirror, looking deep in myself, challenging my confidence and questioning myself. Have this flashback made you weak? Are you going to live the rest of your life with the guilt that you were all ready but still you couldn't help yourself?

NO! A simple NO was my answer to myself without taking any time to think. That NO meant a lot to me and to my life. That NOmade me what i am today.

MORAL

WITH EACH PASSING DAY YOU THINK, YOU FOCUS AND YOU ACHIEVE.

CHAPTER FOUR

EXPECTATIONS

WE OFTEN START TO EXPECT THINGS FROM THE ONE'S WHO ARE IN OUR LIFE, FROM THE ONE'S WHO COME IN OUR LIFE AT A VERY EARLY AGE AND EVEN FROM THE ONE'S WHO COME A MONTH OR A DAY BACK.

WE EXPECT THE UNEXPECTED.

I STILL REMEMBER THE DAY WHEN I LAST EXPECTED SOMETHING. IT WASN'T SOMETHING HUGE OR GRAND. IT WASN'T SOMETHING EXPENSIVE EITHER. IT WASN'T SOMETHING I DIDN'T DESERVE.

CAN ANYONE OF YOU GUESS WHAT IT WAS?

MONEY?

NO.

LOVE?

NO.

CARE?

NO.

SO WHAT WAS IT?

RESPECT.

YES I EXPECTED RESPECT.

FOR ME THIS IS THE MOST EXPENSIVE THING SOMEONE CAN GIVE YOU EVER. MAY BE THAT WAS THE REASON MY EXPECTATION REMAINED AN EXPECTATION. AT ONE POINT, I COMPROMISED MY RESPECT BECAUSE I

WAS AFRAID OF LOSING PEOPLE. I WAS AFRAID OF BEING ALONE. I WAS AFRAID OF EVERY DAMN THING.

EXPECTATION IS A SWEET POISON, YOU WILL ENJOY IT AT FIRST, BUT WITH TIME IT WILL SHOW YOU ITS BAD SIDE. A SIDE I PRAY NO ONE EVER SEES. A SIDE WHICH BREAKS YOU MENTALLY AND EMOTIONALLY. A SIDE WHICH HAUNTS YOU EVEN IN THE DAY TIME. A SIDE WHICH IS EVEN MORE HORRIBLE THAN WE THINK. A SIDE WHICH WILL MAKE YOU LOSE YOUR RESPECT AND DIGNITY.

AND THAT LOSS IS THE HUGE LOSS. THAT LOSS IS NOT THE LOSS OF THE BODY OR MIND BUT IS THE LOSS OF THE SOUL. THAT LOSS IS THE LOSS OF YOUR PEACE. THAT LOSS IS THE LOSS OF YOUR LIFE.

NEVER EVER COMPROMISE YOUR RESPECT.

NEVER EVER EXPECT RESPECT FROM OTHERS.

RESPECT YOURSELF AND RESPECT OTHERS BECAUSE IT IS THE BEST THING YOU CAN

GIVE AND THE HARD THING YOU CAN EXPECT BACK.

GIVE IT ALL WITHOUT ANY EXPECTATIONS.

MORAL...

WITH EACH PASSING DAY YOU EXPECT, YOU BREAK AND YOU BECOME STRONGER.

CHAPTER FIVE

YOU

19th MARCH 2018

I turned myself into a different personality which I never wanted but as it is said “ time and situation teaches us everthing”.

I still remember the day, I was all ready to go out with my family to attend a function. And as usual i got dressed to click some pictures, Clicking Clicking and suddenly I heard a voice.

BISMAAAAA how much more time you are going to take? My mother asked with a full on screaming tone.

Just few more minutes and I am done. I replied.

Can you imagine how it feels to be a different person with a fraction of no time. From one moment of being excited to the next moment of just pretending to be happy and okay, this is how your mental health betrays you, not because it is working that way but because we made some stupid relations to control our moods and lives.

We give authority to some people who always make decisions and things as per thier convinience. It all happened to me just before going out. I started feeling lost even in my home, thousands of thoughts and restlessness was killing me, because the person I ever thought will understand me started misunderstanding me.

And what worst can happen than asked to leave your dream, passion or the goal of you life. It felt like I was asked to die. For sometime it started to feel like my hands slipping away from my dreams, running away from all the milestones I was yet to achieve. I started seeing this nightmare with my eyes wide open.

But NO.

Moving out from stupid relations is fine but moving out from dreams is stupid in itself. I made a decison.

A desicion which no one ever had imagined but yes I did. I broke every realtion who came in between me and my dreams. I made myself heartless for the ones who never thought that my dedication will pay me back ever. That day I was turned to a girl who was never a part of me, who was never meant to be.

I made myself limited to myself, I was extrovert yet introvert. I made friends but there was still no friend of mine. I became my own support and moreover I started believing in my own thoughts and perspectives. I made my rules which were good for me and I made sure that my rules won't harm anyone physically and mentally.

But I feel somethings never fade, somethings never disappear, somethings never leave you. They are meant to remind you all the time what you have gone through, what you have faced and what you have felt. They won't be

remembered as a good book but as a worst nightmare.
Use those incidents in building yourself, use them in creating something best , use them as the same way as you got used at one time, just use them to the fullest. Those incidents will make you strong. Those scars on your body will turn into the brightest stars one could ever see. Those tears will turn out in the oceans of happiness and that will be day you will be proud of what you have survived.

Never let those incidents demotivate you rather get motivated, this life is not limited to only one single person, there will be someone praying for you. There will be someone who will wear your scars as his/her medals, there will be someone who will give you all the happiness you deserve and he will hold your hand and will be proud to have you in whatsoever position you are in. Just believe in this and that day will surely come.

MORAL

With each passing day you try, you believeand you live....

CHAPTER SIX

21-10-2013

THE LAST DAY OF OUR SCHOOL.

I still remember how painful it was to bid goodbye to the ones with whom I have spent my entire childhood. School life for me has been the best of all. A life full of joy, craziness, and naughtiness. And then it was us the 10th class students (SECTION A), the worst batch ever.

How can I forget my all batch mates who have been an equal part in our naughty missions. The mission of throwing bags from the window of our classroom, the mission of irritating BABA SIR, the mission of teasing our Islamiyat teacher, the mission of not attending the school assembly.

And how can I forget that day when I wrote something for the first time in my life and after that, I never looked back. My writing journey started at the end of my school life. But I was satisfied that I took something with me, in me. The story of my friend, a pen and paper, some emotions and feelings running in my veins, with all of this I was all set to go on and on.

School life was over, now it was the time to come out of the pink bubble I used to live in. It was time to come out from the positive world and meet the negative world outside. After school, now it was the time of higher secondary school. The first day of my higher secondary school was a bit confusing and frustrating; it was a mess all around. Maybe I wasn't used to such a life and no one among us usually is. I used to go, attend classes and come back home all alone, but I wasn't aware of one thing, that to survive this part of your life you need to have a big gang with you, a group of fake friends and a swag worth nothing.

I was totally different; I wasn't able to adapt to this phase and then I made my dairy my friend, a real and a pure friend. A friend who was with me in my all goods and bad, a friend who never questioned me, a friend who lived with me and survived with me at the same time.

A friend for life and now "*An essential of life*".

With the end of my school life, I realized that many other things ended too. The essence of true friendship was lost; the pure smile was lost, life in life was lost.

MORAL...

Live your life as you are still in your school days. Never let that child in you be killed by anyone or by you.

With each passing day, you leave places, you enter places and you explore the difference.

CHAPTER SEVEN

GUILT

There are many feelings running down my spine right now and the worst among all of them is feeling GUILTY. I react too much and get angry about things, and later on feel guilty about all that. This feeling is very hard to understand and to live with.

I regret my decisions at sometimes and may be that plays a vital role in making me feel guilty about anything happened earlier. This feeling has been a great trouble for me. A trouble where i am stuck like anything and can't focus on things peacefully.

Guilt is a very powerful emotion, it takes us somewhere else mentally and emotionally. May be sometimes things happen because they were meant to happen and are not in our control, but later on we realize that we make our points more dominating and while doing so we suppressed someone's.

Guilt over power you because you let the negative things overcome your positive things. We need to trust our actions if they are right. we shouldn't blame ourselves rather trust and let this feeling go away. May be sometimes you need to speak about it to feel relaxed or just simply write what you are going through.

Forgive yourself and let your mind and soul heal. Use this guilt and get inspired by it, choose to become a better person with time and situation. It teaches us a lot, it teaches us to be polite with our judgments.

Remember the things you did right with you and with the others too. Those memories are even more worth to appreciate and paying attention to. Look at the bigger picture always. The moment or the phase you are guilty about something is just a part of the life, not the whole life.

Start a new journey with whole heart, a heart full of love, care, respect and free from all kind of guilt's. That is the way you can come out of this feeling and can make your life worth living.

Face yourself in the mirror even when are guilty, even when looking at yourself will make you cry, scream and shatter, but never lose hope, never get demotivated.

Go on you have a beautiful life to live.

MORAL...

WITH ALL YOUR PLUS POINTS BE BRAVE ENOUGH TO SHOW YOUR MINUS POINTS.

CHAPTER EIGHT

CHANGE (A SIMPLE CHANGE OR A REALITY)

With time I understood the difference between being loved and being tolerated. People come, stay and leave according to their needs and moods. People appreciate your efforts, they enjoy your company and with time they start to feel suffocated because you start to give them the place they don't deserve in actual.

And you know what the crazy part is?

You value those people with all the heart and soul, you start to share your highs and lows, ups and downs in such a less time that you even don't bother about your self-respect and your individuality. You make them feel like they have all the rights to rule you, to make you feel worthless and to make you question your own identity and opinions.

The love you shower on them eventually turns to nothing less than suffocation. The care you provide starts to feel like a prison or a cage. People might not understand how to deal with such emotions because they usually try to be the real one in the fake one.

Time has taught me that no matter how much you try to make something happen it won't until and unless the other one isn't equally contributing towards a relationship. No matter how much you value things that won't matter if the opposite one is not willing to value you. No matter how hard you try to sort out the things and situations it won't help until and unless the other one is not real enough to appreciate you and your thoughts.

Time teaches us everything and indeed is the best teacher. A teacher who dies the moment you die. A teacher with you and within you.

Appreciate the time you have here, appreciate each moment and minute.

MORAL

Give out the love in the purest of form, give it all, and give it to everyone.

With each passing day you feel the difference, you get to know things and you smile, yes you smile.

CHAPTER NINE

COMPROMISE AND SACRIFICE

And for him it was easy to share each and everything and for me it was equally difficult. May be at times or most of the times I am not able to make my part clear or make people understand what I want to convey or what I feel.

For me life is good and satisfying until you don't have to struggle about what you want to achieve and what arc your views about anything. For me I am at peace when I can make the opposite person understand my perspective not because I want to change their but I don't want to keep any grudge or confusion in my relationship let it be professional or personal.

I believe that there comes a time in our life where you no longer do things to satisfy your own self but to satisfy others. You gradually start to compromise things just to keep a relationship going or because you have the fear of losing people.

But for me compromise is never an option and it shouldn't be. You need to do things because you want to not because you are obligated to do so. Compromise makes a relationship weak and bounded to four walls. It keeps you away from the person and from yourself as well. Compromise is nothing less than a sacrifice you do hardheartedly, halfheartedly or sometimes you don't know why you do such things or sacrifices.

Love must remain love without any artificial feeling in it. Love must make you strong with each passing day rather than making you weak. It must make you feel higher in the skies rather than dragging you down on the streets. It must make you meet your best version rather than making you lose your individuality. It must empower you with each passing moment rather than making you feel to doubt your capabilities and dreams.

When I love someone I love them. There is no other thing in it. There is just love and love. No compromises, no sacrifices and no halfheartedly things or actions are present there. And I truly believe that we all must love in such a way, that we would be proud. Love isn't meant for compromise.

Love is love.

Simple, sweet and soulful.

MORAL...

WITH EACH PASSING DAY YOU COMPROMISE, YOU SACRIFICE AND YOU LOSE THE ESSENCE OF TRUE LOVE.

CHAPTER TEN

SUICIDE

11th February 2018

With a fraction of no time life skips from your hand, you let it go and you are the one responsible for what you do with your life.

A moment before talking to my friends to the next moment struggling between life and death, this is how we sometimes play with our life. Just because we are not strong enough to control our emotions and most importantly the pain in our life. We don't know how to react to the things happening to us for the first time, the things that break us in just one go. Those things come with no warning, no letter or no appointment.

Committing suicide is a horrible thing you can ever do to yourself. But when you are in that zone nothing else makes sense to you. I still remember that time, it was exactly 11:15 AM in the morning, something happened and I went out of my mind. I saw nothing but a bus coming with full speed and in the next moment nothing was visible to me.

I don't know what happened, how it happened and what was even happening after that. What I know is that I opened my eyes after 5 days of that accident or let's say attempt to suicide. Just after I opened my eyes what were visible to me were my parents crying. I was all covered in white bandage. I was nothing but a dead body laid there on the bed. Having no energy to utter a word or to open my eyes wide.

I was helpless even when everyone there was helping me out. I still remember the words one of the doctors said to me *"you are very lucky, trust me"*.

Why? I asked.

"I haven't seen someone surviving after such major injuries on his/her body. You definitely are

very close to the Allah; he saved you because he wanted to, nothing of our efforts work there. Take good care of yourself". "He replied and left".

Moral....

This life is indeed temporary but is never in our hands. ALLAH is the one and only who can give it to you and take it away from you. You have no right over it.

Appreciate your life, appreciate the blessings he has blessed you with and appreciate the things and persons you have in your life before they leave you not because they want to but because ALLAH decides to take them away.

CHAPTER ELEVEN

THE TWO PERFECT GUYS IN MY LIFE

For me the perfect man of my life is first my father than my brother. Whenever I see them I could feel the true meaning of perfection and the true form of love, care and responsibilities.

From teaching me how to crawl, then walk and then to stand up on my own without any support, he always made sure to make me more strong and independent. He gave his all efforts to make me a better and the best person he could ever see. His sacrifices are worth remembering, the sacrifices he made to make my life easy and secure.

My dreams have always been on priority in my family, my father has supported me in all my decisions and has sometimes even corrected me when wrong, and that was his responsibility which I sometimes lacked to understand. But besides everything he always made sure that I live my life to the fullest with peace and happiness.

From, giving me the better education, then better lifestyle and most importantly the better manners and etiquette, he fulfilled his all the duties in such a way that he has become the meaning of perfection in my life.

Brother, my second father.

From irritating me to teaching me the difference between the right and wrong, he became the second perfect man of my life. Sometimes I misunderstood his actions with restrictions but with time I realized that it is his duty to check and guide me wherever I am wrong. With time I came to know that how some of the responsibilities of my father has got divided, and has now came upon my brother.

Even not being here with me my brother has been with me, within me all the time. We fight a lot but that won't change the fact that how much we love each other.

And no matter what, these two perfect mans have always made sure that all of my wishes were fulfilled.

I see perfection in them; I see my world in them.

Moral...

With each passing day you fight with your family, you misunderstand them but at the end you are incomplete without them.

CHAPTER TWELVE

LOVE OR SUFFOCATION"

Sometimes we don't understand the amount of love,care and respect we give to someone without actually knowing whether the opposite person is capable of taking it or not. We lack to understand that not everybody has same taste, same opinions, same way of reacting or the same way of loving.

I personally believe in whole: instead of some, few, tiny or anything that represents something below over the top. When i give i give it from my soul without keeping anything back in store because i believe the more we give the greater it comes again within.

But sometimes giving too much can harm your own soul, it can damage your body, destroy

your existence and can make you feel useless, worthless and what not. There is nothing wrong with such people who love unconditionally it is just they don't get treated the same way, by the same amount of excitemnet, love and energy.

I remember how I used to love without boundaries, how I used to care as a parent even how I used to hang around as the coolest friend you can ever have but all you need is a couple of heartbreaks, ignorance and disrespect and it is over. Love is the best feeling until you are not making it a responsblity or a liablilty on the other person. Just because you love someone does not mean he or she is ordered with some rules or terms and conditions.

Love is when things happen because you make them happen, not when you have to ask for it. Love is about how you explore eachother without altering each other. love is about the memories you make and even are palnning to make rather than questioning each other for the opinions you don't match. love is all about respecting each others indivisduality and letting them free not because there absence wont affect but because their happiness matters. Love is something eternal which no defintion can define. It is something that will help you to prosper, love never demotivates you, it never make you sad, depressed or a person who no longer has ambitions and dreams.

But the moment you start feel suffocating in a relationship is the time where you must know that you actually lost the essence of real love. You made the love so toxic by your actions, reactions and words that finally you are not giving upon a relation but the relation is giving upon you. you make love a cage, a prison, you make it more than a war one is fighting. and sorry but love is never a war but is the never ending fairy tale where you discover dreams, walk through the paths holding hands, enjoy the moment without any second thought.

And there is no better option than letting it go instead of holding on, as there is nothing left to hold on. The moment you realise that this relation is troubling you or is the hindrance in the way of your happiness is the time where you actually had moved on, then it is just a verbal statement left to make but the actaul decision was already made back in the mind. And it is good to let it go for each others happiness rather than hurting each other in new and different ways again.

Moral

We are happy until we keep love as love, simply love. No additions , no alterations in it. We need to understand the imporatnce of conversation at the right time. Because when you love someone you will always make a way back in instead of making a way out...

With each passing day we understand, we prosper and we love, we love unconditionally.....

CHAPTER THIRTEEN

GUARDIAN ANGEL

We all have some friends, supporters and well wishers in our lives, I too had few. But the best was when I found a guardian angel in my life. Guardian angel is actually not my term but his, but I could not find any better term to describe him in my story so I took it (copywrite given) LAUGHS.

I never imagined that a guy from a random live session would become so important in my life, that he could really make a difference from the rest. A guy with a cute and innocent smile catched my attention when I joined a live session of my friend. We used to chit chat in those live sessions, it was a full package of little music, poetry and limitless fun moments we used to experience. He seemed to be a kind off introvert as he used to talk very less. So, we hardly had any conversation during that time.

It was 28th may 2021, the live session started and he was not there, and one of his friend said that there are some issues he cant come today, and that was the day I texted him for the first time asking is everyhing ok? And the conversation started and kept on going until we heard the AZAAN in the morning. It was not something intentional, it was something which was meant to be. I believe that what happened and how it happened was all scripted by the Almighty, indeed it is.

And this was the best thing happened to me in 2021, he was such a great human being, with amazing thoughts, clear logics. A hard working mature man who knows the difference between right and wrong, who knows the responsblities, importance of family, in short I can say he was an exceptional case in todays world. Apart from all this I will not leave a chance to say how crazy, naughty and crack minded person he is. A guy who is always upto something wild, irritating others to a level where we either want to kill him or get killed, LAUGHS.

Chit chats got stronger and meetings were planned, the deatiled conversation we had, standing in the rain for hours. I was wearing his slippers and he was barefooted, but I did asked you to wear, you denied, so dont blame me for that, LAUGHS... The time we had, was priceless and no matter how much we will enjoy now or in future that feeling, that day will be still on the top. And after that meeting it was quite obvious for both of us, about the bond we created, how comfortable we are with each other, how crazy we are and how crazy we are going to be. We call it friendship, a true friendship today's world has lost somewhere. A friendship which made me a better person.

My guardian angel from then has never let a single day in my life to be boring. He has filled my life with joy, happiness, craziness and abundance of love. Instead of knowing all my mood swings he somehow manages to come over that, he is simply an angel in my life. When he is with me everything is sorted, beautiful, exciting, the aura is positive. Being my guardian angel, he has also been the great critic in my life so that he could make me and my points more clear and logical.

He is insane at times, but that is something I can let go, no matter how hard we fight. I will always let go these small things because there is lot more to appreciate in you rather than holding on to something that is worthless and makes no sense. But to be honest I love fighting with you because you dont know how to win an arguement...laughs... but now have learned some.

I am lucky to have such a cute, sweet and adorable guardian angel in my life (ALHAMDULILAH)

MORAL

People come and go in your life, but understand the worth of worthy people. Appreciate them before you have to appreciate the memories left.

With each passing day we make it for a day, for a year and than forever.......

CHAPTER FOURTEEN

FIND ME IN YOUR MEMORIES

A beautiful yet incomplete morning came up with new experiments, tasks, hurdles and moreover an oppurtunity. Just looking deep into the water and the music high on the earphones I couldn't sense anything but some bitter statements striking my ears again and again with the same intensity as someone was saying it again.

Hey! Do you know where is this cafe located? A random guy tapped my shoulder.

Sorry what i couldn't hear you, with the shivering hands i took off my earphones.

I said do you know where is this place? He showed a picture.

Sorry I have no idea about this place, I replied and left the place.

While moving back I was quite upset not because that guy distracted me from soemthing but actuaaly not giving him an appropriate answer.

I felt guilty that i lied to him about not knowing that place, Yeah I knew where that place is?

But may be my mind was not processing the whole situation at that particular time, May be my soul was not allowing me to remind of that place, may be I just wanted to escape from that thought or something I didn't want to remember, recall or relive.

10th October 2018

A Beautiful day, a beautiful place, and a cup of coffee in my hands I was all ready to finally meet him after 3 odd years. The feeling was so much special that it could be hardly written down or expressed. Love take you up in the skies with such power that we try to believe that we belong to the open sky, but the reality is its just the matter of time and feelings we are in and when the things start to fade away, you are slowly slowly brought down to the land and thrown away.

Finally we were together, sharing same place, time and food. It was nothing less than a dream. I was contineously talking and talking without any pause beacuse of the excitement and love that I just got lost in the moment.

I am getting late. He said.

With a sudden pause I stopped.

I think we are done with this meeting. We should leave now, you must be running late too?

With eyes full of confusion, heart full of anxiety and a shivering body, I was not able to utter a word.

I want you to stay for a while, Can you? I asked with the eyes full of tears.

I have to meet my girlfriend, she is waiting for a long now. He replied.

Girlfriend? I questioned.

Yes, we are getting engagged in a day or two. He added.

For some time my brain stopped working, it stopped to process the words he was saying out loud.

While he was leaving that place, I held the sleeve of his shirt and gave him a ring that I was planning to give him in a much special and a peaceful situation. With no more pain or tears in my eyes I said a Goodbye to him with all the love i carried and all the love I burried. I accepted that it takes greater love to let go than to hold on.

I was at peace because my love was happy with the one he loved, and I was happy because I understood that "You don't have to be there in someone's life, you could be there with them also as a memory.

Moral

With each passing day, we make promises, we break them and we become a memory.

CHAPTER FIFTEEN

I MADE MY OWN FAMILY

One morning I was walking alone. While passing through a road I stopped when I saw a sign board that said, 'humans for sale'. After hesitating for sometime, I made up my mind and entered the shop. I checked with the storekeeper about the price of the humans. The price was between 30 and 50 lakhs. I said to the storekeeper that , "I have only two and a half lakhs with me. Can I take a look at your humans which are on sale?" Sure," the man said and whistled. Five old and weak uncle and auties came out from the room, I was so confused to understand what is all going on. I ended up asking one lady from them.

Why are you on sale? I asked.

The other lady came and said, we are left by our children because they settled their lives either with their wives or in the abroad. We are nothing but a burden on them. So we have decided to sell our selves to the people who wants to buy us and the money we get, we have decided to donate that to make a old age home in the society.

I was shocked, my heart started aching, and my soul teared apart.

I wanted to buy them all rather I wanted to keep them all but the storekeeper was willing to give it for free. No I will pay. I said fiercely, "No, I do not want them for free. They all are precious in this cruel and filthy world, they are so pure that no amount of money would do justice to their worth.. I shall pay in full, Now, I wilI pay whatever I have on hand, and the rest in monthly installments.

The store keeper was curious now. Why do you want to them that cannot run and play with you or benifit you with anything?" I quietly showed him my family picture, they are my grandparents but they are no more in this world. I didn't get the love and affection from them. That is why I want to make them my family and be their family as well.

This was me and my take and that does not mean all those who suffer will care about others. If that were the case, so much suffering would have been wiped off the face of this earth. The ones with problems become so absorbed in themselves and focus only on their lives. In the intensity of their sorrows they fail to reach out to others. If only, we turn towards others and do what we can for them, we would feel the burden within us becoming lighter.

When the problems and sorrows of life overwhelm us, We fail to notice the suffering of a fellow being, be it a lame puppy or a little girl or the old people. It would be nice, if we can offer them a kind word or do a kind deed.

Moral

With each passing day, we are born, we grow old and we are either celebrated to just dropped in a old age home.

Appreciate your parents not when you need them but when they need you the most.

CHAPTER SIXTEEN

FOREVER IS A LIE

What is the best lie you remember someone has ever said to you?

Is it something your parents said they will buy you the toys you wanted in your childhood?

Or is it something your siblings promised to take you out for a picnic?

Your friends lied to you about not calling or texting?

Or your partner lied about not remembering your birthday?

But you know what, the greatest and the biggest lie for me is not a statemnet but a single word.

Yesss a single word, and that word is FOREVER.

I believe as time goes on people kind of reveal themselves in something we never imagined, we never thought, we never wanted to accept. People who started loving you for the behaviour and the nature you carry, the same seems childish to them at a certain time. and what can be more worst than that, worst than accepting someone in a way and than judging them for the same.

I remember the days when I used to be a jolly girl, living my dreams, following my passion, chasing the goals and targets, yet adventerous and childish that no one could be able to define my personality. Yeah may be I had a multiple personality disorder (LOL)

I was a girl who enjoyed life the most in its possible ways as well as impossible ways, I got loved for the same. I believd in relations I made, so I used to give my 100% in anything I was into. That was life for me. But not all people come in your life with the thought of staying, with the mind of positivity and with the soul of peace.

There came a time in my life where I sacrificed almost my dream for a relation, for a person whom I loved the most, not because I couldn't get anyone else but because the soul accepted his aura in a way that it was now going to reject any other coming or approaching. We all go through such time in our lives where life seems to be a fairy tale, love seems to be a bollywood movie and We the Cindrellas.

We start to make future with the one's who don't deserve our present. Who don't appreciate our presence and our love for them. I was one of those types. I made myself mad in love or we say the blind love. I accepted a person with all his flaws and drawbacks because as we all know " Pyaar andaa hota hai".

But to be honest love is such a beautiful thing until you meet a bad soul with damaged brain. Love is the greatest of all feelings, experiences and what not. I loved a guy with all my heart and what I was gifted with was a promise, " promise of forever". And for a time bieng that promise started making sense to me, I started to feel like I am living the life of Cindrella where my prince charming will take all his efforts to keep me with him forever and ever.

But no.

Nothing such happend, I understood with time that it was just a bad experience of such a pure feeling which is called "LOVE". May be that wasn't my time, that guy was not in my fate, may be someone else was praying for him with more intensity in Dua's. I accepted that no matter what, what is your's will be your's in every situation, every obstacle, every hurdle you may face and each moments you share.

I accepted that not all promises are meant to keep, few are left in the halfway to make us meet ourselves in a better and a wiser way. Love is beautiful, don't curse love just because we didn't got what we wanted to have on our plate. Explore love with the open heart, keep you heart open to love, pain and rejections and only than you would come to know what love means and where it belongs.

Moral

With eaching passing day, We love, We love and We just simply love.

Don't let your soul taste the taste of hatred, keep it pure and keep it open for love.

CHAPTER SEVENTEEN

WORDS OVER WEALTH

Not everyone here needs your money or materialistic things, some are hungry for kind words, an honest ear who can listen them for hours and a pure soul who will not judge someone's body and colour.

While coming back from my college I saw a lady sitting on the footpath, She was asking for something to everbody who was coming in her way. I got quite restless by seeing her from some meters of distance. I went a little close to her. She was doing some actions to make people understand what she wanted to say as she couldn't speak properly.

I sat next to her and she started talking to me, but it was so unfortunate I wasn't able to understand one single word. With her contineous actions I understood she was asking for a pen and the notebook. I quickly took out my notebook and pen and gave it to her.

With her old wrinkled hands she was writing something and almost after 20 minutes she showed me the notebook where she wrote her name and her qualification. I was amazed to know she was a graduate and how can I forget her name "ZAMROODA BEGUM".

The conversation started, I turned the page and I asked her why is she like this? Where does she live and Where are her children?

I live in a big house, my husband died because of the heart attack, I have children as well as grand children. She wrote.

Than why are you here on the road?

I want to talk, due to multiple health issues I got some vocal problems and I cannot speak properly from then and nobody can understand what I am saying.

You should stay at home and talk to your children like you are talking to me?

They all are busy with their lives, they find it boring to write down things for me. They have kept a maid who gives me food, wash my clothes. I want to talk that is why I ask people to just sit and listen to me. I want to scream and cry but my voice gets unheard and people think I am asking them for the money. I don't need it. I need a shoulder to keep my head on, an ear who will listen me, a pen and paper so that I can express what is there in my heart from so many years.

While reading all this I was not in my control, I started crying in the middle of the road. And she cried with me too.

It is rightly said, "If anyone gives penny to a poor man, he will get six blessing. But, if you say a kind word to him, you will get thousand blessings.

Don't we long for love and recognition ourselves. Our life feels complete, when we are loved and listened. We need not wait until death to recognize the value of love and service to others. We need to be as excited about giving

as receiving. The door to greatness is giving. Being kind and loving to others is as good as helping others.

Moral

With eaching passing day We listen, We cry and We start to be kind.

CHAPTER EIGHTEEN

KILL YOUR ANGER

Anger is normal, usually healthy human emotion, as long as you have a handle on it. In fact, a certain amount of anger is necessary for our survival. But, when anger spirals beyond control, it can intertere with work, personal relationships and the overall quality of life. People with a short fuse can make life hell for people around them, families and friends are the worst affected. A little moment sometimes causes a lifetime of damage and remorse.

We must remember that no one or nothing can really make us angry, if we don't want to be. You can choose something better and productive. The choice is entirely yours. No one can really make us angry. People can say and do things to us, but it is still up to us as individuals to choose our response to the situation.

Remembering a previous situation when anger did more damage than good, can help us rein in our anger. We can then direct the anger on some constructive task like rearranging a closet, doing the laundry, or taking the dog out for a walk, gardening. anything at all that can help let off steam. Even deep breathing helps, The rationalization can start once the moment of anger has passed. When you are in a calmer state of mind, you can start analyzing and disseminating the various aspects of what angered you. If none of this works, you can seek professional help to manage your anger.

The first step is perhaps the most difficult...making the choice to be free from anger. With determination and God's help, we can try to kill anger before it kills us. The parents whose anger makes the lives of their children miserable and children who burn their parents in anger are also not strangers to us. Often do we see the bitter consequences of anger in personal and public life. Still do we sincerely do anything to get rid of or even control our anger?

If we are aware of our human quality and have real insight and self respect we shall soon realize that anger does not make us. On the other hand if we don't properly value ours as well as other people's personalities we won't feel sorry and ashamed of our anger. If we are wise and intelligent we shall try to restrain our anger. For, anger is such an evil that deprives us of all our human quality. It is true that we may justify our anger if we have a real cause for it. Still we are to ask ourselves if we should become angry, for, anger does no good. It may even make an adverse effect.

Let us try to control our anger. If we cannot do it all by ourselves let us not delay in seeking God's help.

Moral

With each passing We control, We seek help and We over come.

CHAPTER NINETEEN

CARPE DIEM

On one day enjoying life to the next day on the bed in the hospital. This is how life is unpredictable.

This is actually life where all your plans, meetings and what not remains on side and you are brought to a different site all of a sudden.

Life happened to me for the first time and at that time when I was not mentally prepared for it and where I was not aware of what actually life was.

A simple laproscopic surgery turned to be the most worst phase of my life at first, but than I accepted it and took it as a blessing. But during that time, the time itself was tough, harsh, cruel and what not. The girl who was afraid of a prick had to go under such painful phases and treatments that she would not have ever imagined in her worst nightmares.

Those sleepless nights, painful procedures, negative thoughts was killing me inside. I remember how I used to google everything about the medical terms, the medicines and everything. The thought of getting better was like a dream to me because I was so demotivated that I couldn't see any positive things around.

The day I got admitted in the hospital for the second time after my first surgery, I remember the doctor came and told me that you are having 99% chances of second surgery and that is when I lost every hope of positivity not because it was something non curable but I was not brave enough to accept this bitter reality. I cried. I cried without bothering about the other patients or the people around and then there was my sister always there. She came and laughed and said why are you crying? Doctor said you have 99% chances of surgery but there is still that 1% which you are not counting. Keep your faith on that 1% and see how that will help you to help your ownself.

I started thinking the same way and to be honest that line literally helped me while in the hospital as well as after the discharge. Yeah I was discharged from hospital with 2 drains in my abdomen, and that was something very hard to accept that I had to keep them for more time until I will be stable. I was told to come for weekly check ups.

The frequent blood tests and ultra sounds I was supposed to do in the time became a part of life, I used to think when will be that day where I will be finally free from all this? But there was no escape to this situation, willingly or not willingly I had to do all this for my own betterment. The reports used to come normal and I remember the doctor said that we are shocked that how is it possible in a patient like you that the reports are coming out so normal and it is really hard to digest this. And than they told me to do MRCP for the better images of internal organs and he added as per your reports there are chances may be you won't need any second surgery. I was happy, like I was flying I called my sister from the hospital and I shared this with her. There was now a hope that yeah there are chances that I will be fine without any further pain.

I did my MRCP test and after 2 days we went to the doctor showed him the reports and he said that we don't have anything to discuss I just have to give you a date for your second surgery. Honestly I cried, I was so so upset that I didn't talk to my parents for the whole time we were in the hospital or in the way. For 2-3 days I cried and cried my family was contineously counselling me , telling me that everything is going to be fine. But it took me sometime to accept and finally I accepted because very lately I understood that whatever happened was because Allah wanted it to be this way.
He could have made it easier, He could have made it pain free but in that case I would not have learnt what he was making me learn. I

would not have been able to build this patience in myself. I would not have been able to recognize the true well wishers in my life, I would not have been able to appreciate my parents , my siblings, I would not have been able to understand the priorities, I would not have been able to know or understand what faith actually means.

I went through a lot even after knowing that now I have to undergo second surgery I was more relaxed because things now made sense to me. I no longer started to take it as my bad luck but as a lesson from the Almighty. And who can be the best teacher but Allah. I took it as a blessing. I took it with more pride. Because I started to believe that whatever happened or is happening or will happen is because allah wants it. And whatever he plans is the best for us. Indeed he is the best planner.

Moral

We need to understand that what we plan is nothing but a dream but what Allah plans is the real world. We need to start appreciating good health which we don't do while wear are okay, but by the time we even get a simple cold we understand what health means. Appreciate the real people in your life. Appreaciate your family, the ones who stood by you at the times you need them not the times they needed you. Appreciate the realtions you make with people which are beyond blood, materialism,

sympathy, duty, liablity or anything but they mean world to you and they made your life beautiful.

With each passing day

WE FAIL

WE FALL

AND

WE FLY

CHAPTER TWENTY

START TO END

It will start with the big things, like their seat next to you everywhere or their name next to yours on the last pages of notebooks or having the long list of similarities.

And then suddenly all the little things will fade too. You won't remember the sound of their voice in the morning or how their hand felt in yours. You won't remember all the tiny details of every date you had or all the conversations you shared late at night. And then one day someone will ask you their favourite colour, and you'll hesitate..

Till Eternity

This life is may be limited to us. This life is may be not what we wanted it to be.

May be nothing goes according to what we planned but yes this life wouldn't have been life, if you wouldn't have happened to me. I am still happy with this incomplete life because I completely lived it even when there was no shoulder to cry on, no hand to hold, no steps matching mine, no dates and no conversations.

I lived you more than I ever lived life.

May be you were the Life of my Life'

9 798887 726601

Printed by Libri Plureos GmbH in Hamburg,
Germany